UNDERSTANDING CHINA'S CRACKDOWN ON RIGHTS ADVOCATES: PERSONAL ACCOUNTS AND PERSPECTIVES

HEARING

BEFORE THE

CONGRESSIONAL-EXECUTIVE COMMISSION ON CHINA

ONE HUNDRED THIRTEENTH CONGRESS

SECOND SESSION

APRIL 8, 2014

Printed for the use of the Congressional-Executive Commission on China

Available via the World Wide Web: http://www.cecc.gov

U.S. GOVERNMENT PRINTING OFFICE

87–705 PDF   WASHINGTON : 2014

For sale by the Superintendent of Documents, U.S. Government Printing Office
Internet: bookstore.gpo.gov   Phone: toll free (866) 512–1800; DC area (202) 512–1800
Fax: (202) 512–2104   Mail: Stop IDCC, Washington, DC 20402–0001

CONTENTS

STATEMENTS

APPENDIX

PREPARED STATEMENTS

UNDERSTANDING CHINA'S CRACKDOWN ON RIGHTS ADVOCATES: PERSONAL ACCOUNTS AND PERSPECTIVES

TUESDAY, APRIL 8, 2014

CONGRESSIONAL-EXECUTIVE
COMMISSION ON CHINA,
Washington, DC.

The hearing was convened, pursuant to notice, at 3:38 p.m., in room 418 Russell Senate Office Building, Senator Sherrod Brown, Chairman, presiding.

Present: Representatives Robert Pittenger and Tim Walz.

OPENING STATEMENT OF HON. SHERROD BROWN, A U.S. SENATOR FROM OHIO; CHAIRMAN, CONGRESSIONAL–EXECUTIVE COMMISSION ON CHINA

Chairman BROWN. Thank you all for joining us. To all four witnesses, thank you especially for speaking out, and for your courage.

On February 21, 2014, nine members of this Commission, Democrats and Republicans from both the House and the Senate—and you will see that generally in the work of this Commission. It is bicameral, it is bipartisan. There is perhaps more agreement on this Commission than almost any committee in the Congress.

We sent a letter to Chinese President Xi Jinping urging him to end the crackdown on rights advocates in China. Among the cases we highlighted was that of Uyghur scholar Ilham Tohti, and his daughter joins us today. Mr. Tohti is a thoughtful and peaceful advocate of the rights of the Uyghur minority who has sought to build bridges among ethnic groups. We are grateful that his daughter joined us today. Thank you again, Ms. Ilham.

We are grateful that the prominent human rights lawyer Teng Biao could join us via Skype. Teng Biao has provided legal assistance in human rights cases at great risk to himself. Our staff has made every effort to ensure the security of this feed and we hope there will be no disruption.

We are grateful, too, that Mr. Clarke and Ms. Richardson could take time out of their busy schedules to be here. Ms. Richardson is a respected expert on human rights. Mr. Clarke has done considerable research into understanding China's legal reform and rule-of-law development.

The hearing comes at an important time. President Xi Jinping has been in power more than a year. As we'll learn more today, he has presided over a worrisome crackdown that is estimated to have swept away more than 150 activists and lawyers and journalists and intellectuals.

President Xi spoke of respecting the constitution and rule of law when he entered office. He has talked tough on corruption. His government has pledged to protect ethnic minorities. But when his own citizens, including the father of our witness today, sought to hold the Chinese Government accountable they were punished.

They include the legal advocate Xu Zhiyong, who has sought to promote educational opportunity and transparency of officials' finances. He is now serving a four-year sentence for "disturbing social order." They include the activist Cao Shunli, who sought to participate in the drafting of China's human rights report to be presented to the UN Human Rights Council. She died last month after being detained and denied medical treatment.

They include the four lawyers trying to defend Falun Gong members held in illegal detention centers known as black jails. The lawyers have been detained and beaten. During President Xi's first year in office, we have learned that independent voices, even those that echo the government's concerns and try to uphold the law, will not be tolerated.

These actions are not befitting a country that every day claims to want, and is seeking in fact, greater international legitimacy. We urge the government of the People's Republic of China to respect the fundamental rights of every one of its citizens to freedom of expression and press and association and religion.

We do so not simply because this is China's obligation under international law, but because China will be better and stronger if it gives citizens a voice and a stake in the system.

By listening to and respecting the rights of citizens like Ilham Tohti and Xu Zhiyong, China can involve all its people in dealing with the most important problems of the day, corruption, ethnic tensions, and income equality. But first, President Xi and China's leaders must view these citizens not as threats, but as people who want what is best for their country.

I look forward to hearing the witnesses.

Congressman Pittenger, your comments?

[The prepared statement of Senator Brown appears in the appendix.]

STATEMENT OF HON. ROBERT PITTENGER, A U.S. REPRESENTATIVE FROM NORTH CAROLINA; MEMBER, CONGRESSIONAL–EXECUTIVE COMMISSION ON CHINA

Representative PITTENGER. Thank you, Chairman Brown, for calling this important hearing and for allowing me to make an opening statement.

First, I want to thank the witnesses who are appearing before us today, especially Ms. Ilham, who is showing extreme courage coming before us to tell her father's story.

The First Amendment of the U.S. Constitution affords American citizens the rights to freedom of speech, freedom of the press, and freedom to peacefully assemble. These rights are the foundation of what have made our democracy work. These rights are what have allowed for America to continually grow and advance. America must continue to advocate for these rights to be afforded to every person around the world.

Last year, this Commission heard from young women whose fathers had been arrested as political prisoners simply for exercising these rights. Today, we will hear from another young woman who has seen firsthand the repressive tactics of the Chinese Government.

Our job as Commissioners, as Members of Congress, as those who hold the lamp of liberty, must be to continue to bring to light these stories and call for China to end its continued persecution of those law-abiding citizens simply for speaking out on behalf of the oppressed.

Thank you, Mr. Chairman. I look forward to hearing the testimony of the witnesses.

Chairman BROWN. Thank you, Mr. Pittenger, for joining us.

Mr. Walz, thank you for joining us today and your dedication to these causes and these policies that we work on in this Commission, and your involvement in the Commission.

It is my pleasure to introduce the three witnesses. We will hear from each of them, starting with Ms. Ilham. She is the daughter of detained Uyghur scholar Ilham Tohti. Mr. Tohti is a peaceful advocate for the Uyghur community who was arrested in February on charges of separatism. He is a respected economist and writer based at Minzu University in Beijing who was supposed to take up a visiting scholar position at Indiana University last fall. His daughter, Jewher, is now studying English at Indiana University. Welcome. Thank you for being here.

Dr. Teng Biao is a human rights lawyer and scholar. He is a lecturer at China University of Political Science and Law in Beijing. He is now a visiting scholar at the Chinese University of Hong Kong. He has provided counsel on numerous human rights cases and is a co-initiator of the New Citizens' Movement. He is joining us via Skype. Dr. Teng Biao, welcome. Thank you for being here. Apparently it's working.

Donald Clarke is the David Weaver Research Professor of Law at George Washington University Law School. He specializes in modern Chinese law, focusing on corporate governance, Chinese legal institutions, and the legal issues presented by China's economic reforms.

Dr. Sophie Richardson is the China Director of Human Rights Watch. She is the author of numerous articles on domestic Chinese political reform, democratization, and human rights in China, and other countries in Asia. Ms. Richardson, welcome.

Ms. Ilham, welcome. If you would begin your testimony. Thank you.

STATEMENT OF JEWHER ILHAM, DAUGHTER OF DETAINED UYGHUR SCHOLAR ILHAM TOHTI

Ms. ILHAM. Hello. My name is Jewher Ilham and I am a student at Indiana University. I'm grateful for this opportunity to appear here and speak about the suppression of dissent in the People's Republic of China as I have personally experienced it.

Over a year ago, I set out to accompany my father, Ilham Tohti, to the United States, where he was to be a visiting scholar at Indiana University. I was to stay for a month. On February 2, 2013, preparing to depart China, my father and I were detained. Due to a police error, I was allowed to leave. My father was held, beaten, and forbidden from leaving China, all for writing about abuses of civil and religious rights. My father, Ilham Tohti, is a well-known economist and writer based at Central Minzu University in Beijing and an advocate for the human rights of the Uyghur people.

I'm not an academic expert on Xinjiang nor on China's politics, but I have observed the impact of repressive Chinese policies on my own family. 2013 was not the first time my father had been detained and his family harassed. After serious clashes in Xinjiang in 2009 left many people dead and a significant number "disappeared," my father worked to get their names and cast a spotlight on China's repression of Uyghur grievances.

As a result, my family was removed from their residence and moved around for one month. Our phones and computers were confiscated. In April 2011, my father and grandmother were forcibly sent to Guangzhou for a week.

In December 2011, I returned home from school one day to find an empty home. My stepmother, my father, and my brothers had been sent to Hainan for two weeks. In 2012, the authorities blocked my brother from registering for school or having a passport. The university also canceled my father's class for one semester. His Web site was sometimes shut down.

In the fall of 2013, state security personnel rammed my father's car and told him they would kill everyone in our family. But the worst happened after January 15 of this year. A large group of police took my father away without any due process. We had no information about him. His lawyer was denied contact with him. On January 25, the government announced accusations against him, including inciting separatism and hatred of the country, and praising terrorists.

Anyone who knows my father realizes how false these charges are. My father never speaks about separatism. By arresting my father, China has driven Uyghurs to understand that their justified grievances cannot get any sort of hearing. Today, my father is in the Urumchi Municipal Prison, but no one can visit him.

The Chinese state often metes out collective punishment to a prisoner's family. My stepmother has no access to family funds in my father's bank account. She and my young brothers are monitored 24 hours a day. Police sleep outside their door at night and keep watch there during the day.

Phone calls to my stepmother are monitored, making it difficult for her to communicate with me. She may lose her employment due to my father's political imprisonment. My oldest brother has become withdrawn and introverted. Having witnessed our father being taken away, he now has nightmares.

Finally, there are some students of my father who have been arrested and imprisoned too, with very little known as to their whereabouts. China has imprisoned a dissident intellectual whose sole crime was advocating human rights and equitable treatment for the Uyghur people.

I am heartened that the Congressional-Executive Commission on China has taken an interest in my father's case and is seeking to learn more about the facts of his imprisonment. Thank you.

Chairman BROWN. Thank you very much, Ms. Ilham. We really do appreciate your comments and your joining us.

Dr. Teng Biao will join us via Skype from Hong Kong. Dr. Teng Biao, welcome.

[The prepared statement of Ms. Ilham appears in the appendix.]

STATEMENT OF TENG BIAO, HUMAN RIGHTS LAWYER AND SCHOLAR (via Skype)

Mr. TENG. Thank you. Just before the First Lady Michelle Obama gave a talk at the Peking University, I tweeted to draw her attention to the plight of two remarkable Peking University alumni—Cao Shunli and Xu Zhiyong. For the past 10 years, Dr. Xu Zhiyong has become one of the most prominent figures in the human rights movement.

The last time I was in contact with him was a few days before he was arrested. He sent a record of his conversation with the secret police. The government gave him several opportunities to compromise. If he agreed to abandon the New Citizens' Movement, he would not be put into prison. But Dr. Xu refused to compromise; he was sentenced to four years.

This past year at least 200 human rights defenders have been arrested, including one of my best friends, Ilham Tohti. It is confirmed that many activists have been tortured. Many of these people are connected to the New Citizens' Movement. Its earlier incarnation was an NGO founded by Dr. Xu Zhiyong and me in 2003, focusing on freedom of speech, religious freedom, and other constitutional rights.

The New Citizens' Movement encourages people to fight for civil rights and unite rights defenders around the country. These activities include promoting educational equality, pressing officials to disclose their assets, and arranging same-city dinner gatherings. By using online mobilization, street speeches, and peaceful protests, the New Citizens' Movement has brought the Rights Defense Movement to a new height.

Why is the Chinese Government savagely suppressing rights defenders? For the past 10 years, the Rights Defense Movement has made great progress. Thanks to our struggles and sacrifice, we have seen several changes. First, the movement is growing from individual cases to street activities; second, from online activities into real-world activities; third, from legal appeals toward political appeals; fourth, from individual to organized activism.

Then the authorities sense an obvious threat. However, the rulers of China refuse to engage in dialogue with civil society and brutally punish anyone who dared to threaten their rule.

Nonetheless, more and more people are standing up to demand rights and democracy. For example, recently in Jiansanjiang, several lawyers were detained for investigating a "legal education center"—or "brainwashing" classes? Why did they stand up to disclose "brainwashing" classes? Because they are the concentration camps of today. Countless Falun Gong practitioners have been sent to these "brainwashing" classes. At least 3,000 have been tortured to death.

As a result of fighting for freedom, many lose their own freedom. I recall the time in 2011 when Beijing's secret police picked me up and put me in solitary confinement for 70 days. While the secret police used violence against me, they declared, "Don't talk about law, no one can help you." But I never gave up hope.

My longing for justice and freedom gave me strength. I believe that our struggle is meaningful and we are becoming more powerful. I also firmly believe that in the United States, in Europe, and in every corner of the world where the light of freedom shines, while the struggle of human dignity continues, we will not be forgotten.

I greatly admire the U.S. Congress and the government for your efforts in advocating freedom and human rights. However, the international pressure on violators of human rights is far from adequate. The Chinese Government not only manipulates the international human rights system, it also makes use of its influence in order to blackmail democratic nations.

How much economic benefit can we sacrifice for freedom? When people make this calculation, they are already on the wrong track. The oppressors of freedom are becoming more powerful by taking advantage of the head-in-the-sand policies of democratic countries and "the silence of the good." Oppressors will not respect national boundaries. By the time the free world feels it needs to protect freedom, I fear it may be too late.

Thank you very much.

Chairman BROWN. Thank you very much, Dr. Teng. We will begin questions in a moment.

Mr. Clarke, thank you for joining us.

[The prepared statement of Mr. Teng appears in the appendix.]

STATEMENT OF DONALD CLARKE, DAVID A. WEAVER RESEARCH PROFESSOR OF LAW, GEORGE WASHINGTON UNIVERSITY SCHOOL OF LAW

Mr. CLARKE. Thank you. Mr. Chairman, members of the Commission, in my testimony today I want to look at two recent detentions in China and discuss their significance for the rule of law in China, and these detentions are those of Xu Zhiyong and Ilham Tohti.

I believe that the main significance of these detentions lies not in the substance of the charges against them—it's not new that China seeks to repress those whom it sees as its enemies—but rather in the process that accompanied the detentions.

Xu Zhiyong's current troubles began when he was placed under an informal kind of house arrest on April 12, 2013; his formal detention did not begin until July 16. After formal detention, the police can stretch out to 30 days the time limit for requesting approval of the next stage, which is the formal stage of arrest. The procuracy, which is the body in charge of prosecutions that approves the arrest, has seven days in which to decide to approve or disapprove the arrest.

In Xu's case, the indictment says he was formally arrested—again, he was already in custody at the time—on August 22, which is exactly 30 days plus 7 days following his formal detention, so apparently someone was keeping a very close eye on the calendar. But to call this arrest lawful we would have to be satisfied that the term during which he was under house arrest prior to his formal detention was lawful.

Now, what about that? The closest thing Chinese law has to house arrest—this term is often used in media descriptions, and indeed one can call it house arrest, but the important thing to understand is that Chinese law does not have really a term they call house arrest—it is an institution called supervised residence, but that has a number of conditions set forth for it in Chinese law, one of which is that in order to put someone under supervised residence, which is essentially house arrest, it must be that the conditions for arrest—that is, this later formal stage—are already deemed satisfied.

So in that case it's impossible to justify Xu's subsequent 37 days in formal detention while they were allegedly deciding whether or not the conditions for arrest were satisfied, because logically they must have already made that decision in order to put him under supervised residence.

Once a suspect is arrested, the authorities have basically up to five months—there are all kinds of ways to extend it up to five months—to keep him in custody while they investigate. Even this five-month limit can be extended indefinitely by action at a very high level. That's the Standing Committee of the National People's Congress, which presumably is very troublesome. Xu was not put on trial until January 22, 2014, exactly five months to the day after his formal arrest.

So again, this suggests that the generous time limits afforded by the Criminal Procedure Law were used to the fullest, something that really shouldn't have been necessary given that the Foreign Ministry has insisted that Xu Zhiyong's case was simply an ordinary criminal case, no politics about it at all.

The trial itself was marred by a number of violations of the letter and spirit of Chinese law. First, it was not in any real sense open, despite the lack of any grounds under Chinese law for closing it. Second, the defense was not permitted to cross-examine any witnesses for the prosecution, despite the rule calling for cross-examination, or at least some way to challenge evidence, in the Criminal Procedure Law. Third, he was not permitted to call his own witnesses. To protest these and other problems, Xu and his counsel elected to remain silent during the hearing. At the end he attempted to make a statement but was cut off by the judge.

Moving on to Professor Tohti: Ilham Tohti was detained on January 15, 2014, and apparently formally arrested on February 20 on a charge of separatism. This period of time between detention and arrest could fit within that allowed under Chinese law if his case is deemed complex. So far, the time between arrest and trial has not been exceeded.

Nevertheless, the state has deprived him of his rights under Chinese law in other ways. On March 4, his lawyer, Li Fangping, stated that he was no longer allowed to communicate with Tohti, apparently the reason given being that state secrets were involved. This is an excuse the Chinese Government has used so often in circumstances where it is highly implausible that it really no longer carries any credibility.

Ms. Ilham has already detailed other problems such as cutting off funds to his wife's bank account and, previous to his detention, of course, taking him on various tours around China paid for by the state that he may not have wanted to take.

So there are two lessons here. First, following legal procedures is of course better than not following legal procedures, but it doesn't necessarily produce justice. We have to ask what the laws say, how they were produced, and who gets to interpret them.

May I have another 30 seconds?

Chairman BROWN. Proceed.

Mr. CLARKE. The second lesson is that the Chinese Government retains its ambivalent attitude toward the values of the rule of law. In many cases it wishes to claim the mantle of fidelity to law. It does so sometimes by making the law vague and flexible enough to achieve its purposes, sometimes simply by falsely claiming to be following law, but at other times it doesn't seem to be trying even to appear to be offering fair proceedings, or at least proceedings that follow its own rules. Sometimes authoritarian states try to turn political issues into legal issues in an attempt to neutralize them. The Chinese state sometimes seem to go out of its way to demonstrate that ostensibly legal issues are really political issues.

So I would end just by saying it's really not clear whether it's reasonable to expect at least a slow movement toward the values of rule of law, especially a process-oriented rule of law.

Thanks for the opportunity to testify. I am sorry for going over.

Chairman BROWN. No problem. Thank you. Thank you, Mr. Clarke.

Mr. CLARKE. I would appreciate any questions.

Chairman BROWN. Thank you.

Dr. Richardson?

[The prepared statement of Mr. Clarke appears in the appendix.]

STATEMENT OF SOPHIE RICHARDSON, CHINA DIRECTOR, HUMAN RIGHTS WATCH

Ms. RICHARDSON. Thanks very much for the opportunity to testify and for your ongoing leadership. Thanks also to your excellent staff and the work they do.

My written remarks summarize some of the background that we've written about the crackdown on Chinese human rights defenders, but here I simply want to stress that even if one isn't concerned about human rights issues, which obviously we think people should be, I think the current crackdown is bad news for reform generally in China.

By that I mean that Xi Jinping has already shown himself to be a hardline and conservative leader in ways that deeply undercut the kind of popular support he is going to need if he wishes to advance the kind of tough, complex reform agenda against deeply vested interests and bureaucratic intransigence. I raise that simply to make the point that, now more than ever, respect by the Chinese Government—or lack thereof—is a bellwether we think for political, economic, and legal reform going forward.

I was asked to focus on three specific issues today. One, about similarities and differences in the current crackdown from past ones. I think the similarities are that these things tend to happen at times of political uncertainty.

At the moment, that really is about the fate of Xi Jinping's reform agenda and about the investigations of individuals like Zhou Yongkang, senior political figures who are now being investigated presumably on corruption charges. I think the other similarity is that the prospects for accountability for the crackdown itself remain quite low. It will be difficult to imagine prosecutions for the people who have abused Xu Zhiyong and Ilham Tohti and who are responsible for Cao Shunli's death.

I think there are a couple of important differences right now. The first one is that I think the current crackdown appears to be considerably more strategic, proactive, and aggressive on the government's part. It's not simply reacting to external events like Liu Xiaobo's 2010 Nobel Prize win. I think we're seeing authorities targeting people who are part of initiatives like the New Citizens' Movement, or going after professors and their students, as has also been the case for Professor Tohti's—some of his students.

Second, the government appears to be trying to break down the interdependent relationships between social media activists and mass media that we think are often critical to actually advancing some kind of change, for example, the push against "Big Vs" last year, against certain kinds of Internet users.

Arguably, of greatest concern, this crackdown is targeting incredibly moderate middle-of-the-road activists and issues. These are people who are pushing for public asset disclosure, for access to education, access to UN human rights mechanisms. These are not particularly incendiary calls for regime change, these are issues that would at best wind up in the B section of most American newspapers. The fact that even those issues are considered off limits is of real concern.

I was asked to say a few words about how Tibetan and Uyghur human rights defenders are faring. Obviously we have talked today about the disastrous and politically motivated prosecution of Ilham Tohti. I am compelled to note that yesterday marked the 12th anniversary in prison of Tenzen Delek Rinpoche. These are communities that are extremely vulnerable.

Alongside the national crackdown, I think the tightening in both of those regions following self-immolations, following the Chinese Government's efforts to paint Uyghurs without providing any credible evidence as responsible for attacks on civilians in Beijing and Kunming, puts those communities at even greater risk and actually lowers the standard of what kind of behavior is considered problematic.

We're keeping a close eye on the case of Abduweli Ayup, who is a Uyghur who was arrested in July 2013 for raising money for schools. He was detained, along with two other men. Nine months later, we still don't even know what the charges against him are and that's a real concern to us.

I want to spend at least a minute talking about what we think the United States should be doing. Despite, I think, the often Herculean efforts of people who spend all day within the U.S. Government trying to defend human rights issues, we think that senior levels of the Administration remain deeply ambivalent about whether human rights issues in China are ones simply to be managed primarily for a domestic constituency or whether they are ones that the United States should be making an effort to try to solve. Those are two very different things.

We all know that change is largely going to come from inside China, but I think there is a role for external pressure, as Professor Teng has noted, and that largely through reputational pressure there should be a price levied against the senior Chinese leadership for these kinds of abuses.

I'm going to try to exercise the same privilege that Professor Clarke did, if you don't mind.

I think helping solve the problem actually requires elevating abuses and individual cases consistently to the senior-most discussions, from the President on through members of the Cabinet, above and beyond the State Department and the usual suspects who are tasked with raising human rights abuses. They should all be prepared to raise an individual case, just one—it's not a big ask, just one—and be prepared to talk about that case when they meet with their Chinese counterparts.

Ask why that person has been detained. Ask why they've been charged with what they've been charged with. Be politely prosecutorial and ask for an explanation. Often Chinese interlocutors aren't going to have an answer on the spot, but certainly the fact that an unusual suspect asked the question will certainly be made note of.

For anybody in the U.S. Government who thinks that human rights issues in China are somehow beyond their bailiwick, I would commend them to Susan Rice's December 2013 speech which made very clear that these issues cut across the bilateral relationship.

I think solving the problem also means using things like the 2011 Executive Order allowing for visa bans. I think solving the problem means the United States, which has generally been good on refuge issues from China, stepping up to counter pressure on Nepal, for example, to forcibly return Tibetans, and on southeast Asian countries to forcibly return Uyghurs.

Last but not least, I think helping solve the problem entails speaking to, for, and about these activists who are running extraordinary risks and paying incredibly high prices for their work. Now, these are the people who are doing what the United States says it wants to see inside China, and I think recognizing that kind of work and credentialling those kinds of people is pivotal to bringing at least a little bit of an end to some of these kinds of problems. Thanks.

[The prepared statement of Ms. Richardson appears in the appendix.]

Chairman BROWN. Thank you, Dr. Richardson.

Ms. Ilham, thank you again for your testimony. You had said that no one can visit your father. Do you know how he's doing, and do you have thoughts on what we can do to help him?

Ms. ILHAM. Until now I didn't get any news about how he is doing because nobody can visit him. And I'm really grateful for what you have been doing about this during these days, and especially for supporting my father's full rights and expressing concern for his current situation. I think I would ask the United States and everyone to continue to press China for his release and not to forget his case. I hope that all efforts can be continued. Thank you.

Chairman BROWN. What is your sense, Ms. Ilham, of the growing violence in Xinjiang?

Ms. ILHAM. I'm sorry?

Chairman BROWN. What is your sense of the growing violence in Xinjiang?

Ms. ILHAM. Well, I'm not an expert, an academic expert on Xinjiang, but I think I, my father, and most of the Uyghur people, I think nobody really wants violence and nobody wants to hurt innocent people. So some people, a few Uyghur people, now use violence but that doesn't mean that everybody wants to do like that. Also, it doesn't mean that my father supports this violence.

Chairman BROWN. Okay. Okay.

Ms. ILHAM. That's what he struggles for, to let people change their mind.

Chairman BROWN. Okay. Thank you, Ms. Ilham.

Dr. Teng, can you describe the New Citizens' Movement in more detail and why should we in the United States be paying attention to the New Citizens' Movement?

Mr. TENG. Yes. The New Citizens' Movement began formally in 2012, and there are hundreds or thousands of Chinese citizens involved in this movement. So we try to unite all citizens with the ideas of the rule of law or liberal democracy, and come together to discuss public affairs.

Since 2003, Dr. Xu and many other human rights lawyers promoted the Rights Defense Movement, and he also initiated the New Citizens' Movement. This movement brought the Rights Defense Movement to a new level. Many human rights activists who are promoters of the New Citizens' Movement are now detained, and it's reported that some of them have been tortured in detention, so I hope the international society can pay more attention to political prisoners and the New Citizens' Movement.

Chairman BROWN. Thank you, Dr. Teng.

Professor Clarke, you followed and have been involved and observed up close China's legal development. Where is it going in the next 5 to 10 years, and what impact and how do we have impact as a Nation in encouraging development of the rule of law in China?

Mr. CLARKE. Well, I think it's not—maybe I could say where it's not going. I don't see it going significantly in the direction of political liberalization. In the Decision of the Third Plenum of the Central Committee which was recently held, there were some legal reforms mentioned that might have some kind of a positive effect, I think, in bringing greater regularity to the court system.

But that would be regularity in enforcing whatever laws happen to be there, so maybe less room for arbitrary discretion by local political leaders and having local courts do what they want, but no limitations, no further limitations on the ability, for example, of the central leadership to, in effect, persecute those that they are interested in persecuting, such as people like Xu Zhiyong and Ilham Tohti. So to sum up, I guess I would say there may be some modest institutional changes that would be consistent with greater protection of human rights but wouldn't necessarily have that content.

Chairman BROWN. Dr. Richardson, what, in light of Professor Clarke's comments about any impact we could have, are our points of leverage to encourage China to improve its human rights behavior, if you will, and to move more toward rule of law?

Ms. RICHARDSON. Well, I think it's at a couple of different levels. The first obviously is really at a diplomatic public/political level. I think that unless the senior leadership knows that they are going to have to answer questions in every single meeting they have with senior American counterparts, then you might get a little bit better behavior.

There are obviously much more systemic problems particularly in the legal system, and especially as long as the CCP [Chinese Communist Party] retains as much control over the legal system as it does. That said, I think there's enormous room to providing support to, for example, innovative lawyers who are trying to either improve particular laws or access to justice, essentially.

Chairman BROWN. But what are Chinese officials saying when we bring that up? Do they accuse us of compromising on voting rights or do they accuse us of checkered racial policies in this country, or do they deny, or do they do all of the above?

Ms. RICHARDSON. It varies a little bit on what the setting is. For example, when the Chinese Government publishes its annual report on the United States' human rights record, that tends to largely be about crime and about racism and certain kinds of systemic discrimination in the United States and it's their way of saying, you know, you have these problems too so stop talking about ours.

Typically what happens if an individual case is raised is that there will sort of be—typically there won't be much of a reply at all, or you'll get a reply to say, you know, this case is—it's a common criminal. This is somebody who has violated Chinese law.

Chairman BROWN. Do you both agree, Professor Clarke and Dr. Richardson, that U.S. Government officials bringing up Ilham's father's case is meaningful and helpful?

Mr. CLARKE. Yes, I would agree. I think that the experience of dissidents in Eastern Europe, for example, as people like Vaclav Havel have testified, is that knowing that the attention of the world was on them was extremely helpful and kept them going.

I think that on the level of the government, too, there's sort of a natural reluctance on a human basis to raise embarrassing, uncomfortable topics. But I don't think it does any harm to do so and I think it may do some good, again, by letting the Chinese Government know that people have not forgotten these issues.

Chairman BROWN. It does not result in more retribution?

Mr. CLARKE. I don't think so.

Chairman BROWN. I'm sorry, that's Dr. Richardson. Either way. Okay.

Ms. RICHARDSON. I agree entirely with what Professor Clarke just said. Typically what happens in especially high-profile political cases is that prison authorities then know that a particular individual is being asked about, and in fact they tend to be treated better.

Chairman BROWN. Okay. Okay.

Mr. Pittenger, your comments please. Your questions. Thank you.

Representative PITTENGER. Thank you, Mr. Chairman.

Ms. Ilham, your father made it clear that he is committed to peaceful dialogue between different ethnic groups in China. Why do you think Chinese officials are so fearful of him that they would lock him up and charge him with such a serious crime as separatism?

Ms. ILHAM. Excuse me. I have a problem for understanding. Can I ask for translation?

Representative PITTENGER. Sure.

Ms. ILHAM. First of all, ethnicity has been a very sensitive topic since a long time ago, and my father is a very outspoken person. He has been speaking about the Uyghur situation in front of the public for a long time. He has been very honestly talking about the situation, the Uyghur situation in China.

Of course they have a good point and they have bad points made. I think in my view, I think Chinese cannot accept that my father is telling the truth. But when my father—he just wants people to know the truth and to get more—like, Uyghur people can have equal human rights like the general Chinese citizen. Thank you.

Representative PITTENGER. He is a very courageous man.

Chinese authorities, Ms. Ilham, have frozen your father's bank accounts. You've spoken about how your two younger brothers have been affected by his arrest.

Ms. ILHAM. Yes.

Representative PITTENGER. Could you talk more about the impact of your father's arrest on your family?

Ms. ILHAM. Well, since January 15, my family has been under house arrest. They have been so for fully 24 hours a day. The police sleep in front of the doors and so the neighbors have really—they have complained and they don't—now they've stopped talking to my family.

Of course, my brothers, their personality has been really affected. They were really extroverted and now they've become introverted. They stopped talking, especially the elder one, my 7-year-old brother, because he saw how my father was beaten and taken away by the police, so he knows what is going on, so now he has—every time when we Skype he tells me he really misses our father and he wants to see me soon.

Also, my brothers—basically, my brothers—like, their school work also has been affected. Until now I didn't see my family for more than one year. I had never left my parents before. Because my elementary school, my middle school, are all very close to my home. This is my first time not seeing my family for such a long time.

Representative PITTENGER. Thank you. We stand with you, certainly.

Ms. ILHAM. Thank you.

Representative PITTENGER. Dr. Teng Biao?

Mr. TENG. Yes.

Representative PITTENGER. Thank you, sir, for your testimony. One of your goals is to combat China's serious corruption problem with the Chinese Government also seems to be trying to address, possibly for political reasons. What do you think needs to happen in order for the Chinese Government to meaningfully address the issue of systemic corruption?

Mr. TENG. We have seen top Chinese leaders also crack down on corruption, even higher level leaders. But we have seen that Dr. Xu Zhiyong and many other human rights activists who demanded disclosure of official assets have been detained and put into prison. They are oppressing other activists who are against corruption.

It is obvious that without meaningful political or judicial reform, without separation of powers and judicial independence, there is no hope to get rid of political corruption. Xi Jinping and the Communist Party is using its power to crack down on civil society and they will not change the political system.

Representative PITTENGER. Dr. Teng Biao, what will it take for the Chinese Government to view the New Citizens' Movement, human rights lawyers, and people like yourself not as threats but rather as well-intentioned citizens who want to help China?

Mr. TENG. I beg your pardon?

Representative PITTENGER. Well, you have spoken previously about the New Citizens' Movement. What I am trying to find out is do they see you as a threat today. What will it take for them to view you differently, to see you as one who is well-intentioned for the best interests of China?

Mr. TENG. I have been kidnapped and detained several times and since I'm a visiting scholar in Hong Kong, they cannot arrest me. Someone told me that I'm also on that list, so if I go back to China, it's highly possible that I will be arrested. But many other human rights defenders and lawyers are still continuing their human rights activities even today, and I will go back to China because it's my responsibility to fight for human rights and freedom in China.

Representative PITTENGER. Thank you, sir.

Last night I had dinner with a major banker with the Ex-Im Bank in China. I discussed with him those who stand for human rights, particularly those who have freedoms of conscious issues and religious freedoms, and particularly Christian people in this country.

My statement to him was that those people of faith were people who would be good citizens because they, as followers of Jesus, would in large measure be honest people and people that would be good for the culture and good for business.

I think that is what I'm trying to understand. You have well-intentioned objectives for the good of China in your movement with the New Citizens' Movement and my hope is at some point that the Chinese Government will see that people like yourself are good for the culture and good for the society.

Mr. Chairman, do I have time for one more?

Chairman BROWN. If you want to ask each of the other two witnesses.

Representative PITTENGER. Yes, I do.

Chairman BROWN. You may proceed.

Representative PITTENGER. Thank you.

Dr. Richardson, thank you for your testimony. I'm working with a former U.S. Ambassador to the United Nations on a separate issue but I'm interested in your perception of how the United Nations is dealing with these issues.

How would you describe China's participation in the United Nations, particularly on the UN Human Rights Council, the universal periodic reviews of each country's human rights record conducted by the UN Human Rights Council, and is the United Nations an effective forum for dealing with China or does it help legitimatize China's abuses?

Ms. RICHARDSON. How much time have I got, sir?

[Laughter].

Ms. RICHARDSON. Let me see if I can organize this. I think in light of the extraordinarily uncooperative performance the Chinese Government turned in around the final phase of its own review under the universal periodic review mechanism, including largely around Cao Shunli's death and the efforts to postpone that session, the efforts to hold it when the translators would have gone home, the extraordinary decision to try, instead of for once objecting to people speaking to staying silent when a number of NGOs wanted to use their speaking opportunities to have a moment of silence to remember Cao Shunli.

I think it shows you not only how the process of many issues at the United Nations essentially becomes the substance for the Chinese delegation in question, but also the lengths that they'll go to to really, I think, prevent scrutiny of particular issues inside the country.

If we're talking about votes on Syria and Libya and how they may or may not react to the proposal of, for example, an ICC [International Criminal Court] referral for North Korea based on the Commission of Inquiry report that was just completed, which is an extraordinary piece of work, I think it's pretty clear that we can expect uncooperative behavior there.

There are a number of different levels we can try to talk about this on, but I think what's most important for defenders inside China—and I obviously welcome other people's views on this—is that the UN's system presents them with a number of mechanisms to at least discuss the country's human rights record. I think in that sense it's important. The government, I think, will continue to pour extraordinary resources into limiting that discussion.

Representative PITTENGER. I thank each of you for your responses and for the opportunity to visit with you. Thank you particularly, Ms. Ilham.

That concludes my questions.

Chairman BROWN. Mr. Pittenger, thank you for your questions. Mr. Walz, welcome.

Representative WALZ. Well, thank you, Mr. Chairman. To my fellow Commissioners and the staff, thank you all for being here.

Ms. Ilham, I noticed and I think your father's about my age and I've got a young daughter. I could only hope that she would be as courageous in a similar situation as you have shown because I think all of us in this room certainly understand what your courage means to you and your family. So with that I'm grateful to you, and I think to each of you.

Dr. Richardson, you've summed this up and you've done a wonderful job, all of you have, of pointing this out. I very much appreciate where you were hitting on. This isn't just an academic exercise. It feels like many of us have been here for so long. Unfortunately, there will be another young lady sitting where Ms. Ilham is with a similar story.

The question that I want to ask each of you, and my colleagues have asked on this, is how do we get at the heart of making that difference? And I get it. You know, this response that you have things you need to work on, heck yeah, we do. But we're not going to cover them up and we're certainly going to discuss them and we're certainly going to move in a direction to try and address those.

So that doesn't get you off the hook. My question is, do any of you feel, and each of my colleagues have asked wonderful questions of where that point of leverage is or whatever, I think many of us still keep coming back to is, do we have the courage on the leverage? Because it's going to come back to economic issues on that. That's going to make the leverage and that's going to hurt if we choose to do so.

Do any of you have confidence that there are those things that are going to make a difference? There's ways that we can go and ways that we can influence that, because I think we've all struggled with this for many years. We've struggled with it prior to most favored nation and decoupling and everything else, and we've struggled since then.

But I, for one, want to know what the path is to move that back in because I am deeply concerned that now the statements you've all made, that we're just not even going to listen to what you say. I think this troubled me, Mr. Clarke, but I think you're right. We're not even making an attempt to say we're doing it anymore at times, we're just going to do it, and that's very challenging.

So I'd just like to hear from each of you. I know this is very broad, but I'm at the point where, what can we do? It sometimes feels very lonely that it's this room, and I'm glad you're here because I know there are others thinking of this and the folks that are here. But what can we do? How do we make a difference?

Ms. RICHARDSON. There are a lot of people out there to support. This is a big and messy answer to a big, broad question. I think there's much to be said for feeding into a sense, particularly on the Chinese Government's part, about needing to compete for a sense of legitimacy. It drives me nuts—nuts—that the United States fails every single time there's a leadership transition to point out that this is not an elected government. Every single time. It's 800 million people who once again got denied the right to vote. The United States comments on transitions and elections all over the world all the time. It treats China differently and it forgets that this is not a government that was elected. There is a real discussion domestically.

Representative WALZ. Why does it forget if it's not economics? Why do you get the pass?

Ms. RICHARDSON. It's inconvenient, it's embarrassing. Who has to do it? There's protocol. I mean, the list of reasons I have for not doing it that I've been given by U.S. Government officials over the years is long.

But look, I mean, Teng Biao is part of an incredible movement of people who are trying. It's a question you precisely asked a few minutes ago about, what does it take for that government to realize that this movement is constructive, that it's meant to better the country, not to threaten it?

So I think really what has to be at the center of efforts is putting the CCP on the back foot to have to answer for its behavior, but also to do the best the United States and other governments can do to recognize people and movements that are actually trying to act legitimately in the interests of larger numbers of people inside China.

It's a big, messy question that doesn't necessarily follow to obvious policy implications. But the United States has to do a much better job in remembering that it's people like Teng Biao who speak a lot more legitimately for people inside China than any of the officials who wind up in meetings day after day after day with U.S. Government officials.

Representative WALZ. Well, if I could follow up, and I appreciate that. Teng Biao, ni hao. Good morning. I know it is 4:30. I want to see that sunrise over the harbor that you're going to see. I'm grateful for you. And you heard Dr. Richardson. Could you elaborate a little bit on that? Because I guess for us this is a group here that cares about this. The Senator has been here for years and moving this ball forward. What can we do to help? What can we constructively do to help?

Mr. TENG. Yes. Thank you. It seems that Chinese leaders never listen to the outside world but the fact is that you, the United States, and the whole world who are fighting for human rights have made a difference. Without your support, we human rights defenders in China will face more difficulty, and we have made a difference, too, in China.

We can see that even though the crackdown never stops, we have seen more and more Chinese people standing up for human rights and freedom, the Internet, civil society, NGOs, the human rights lawyers group, and we have made great progress in civil society. So my idea is don't stop the support for human rights in China; it's always meaningful. So we hope to have more media reports, more statements, more hearings, and mentioning more names, and more support for NGOs. That's very good and we really appreciate it.

Representative WALZ. My time is about up. Maybe Dr. Clarke, or if we come back around on a second.

Chairman BROWN. You'll be presiding so you can do that.

Representative WALZ. Okay. We'll wait until we come back around, Dr. Clarke, on a second one.

Chairman BROWN. Thank you. I was called to vote. I'd like to ask one more question, then turn it over to Congressman Walz to preside. Mr. Pittenger, if you want to stay, certainly.

I was intrigued by the last line of questions on Mr. Pittenger's insight and then Mr. Walz's discussion. Dr. Teng said that "countries like the United States often sacrifice human rights for trade with China." That seemed to be accurate back in 1999–2000 when Congress passed PNTR [permanent normal trade relations]. I remember a friend of mine said there were more corporate jets at National Airport lobbying for PNTR than he had ever seen.

CEOs who normally didn't bother with rank-and-file House Members in the majority or the minority walked the halls of the Cannon, the Rayburn, and the Longworth Building, imploring individual Senators or individual Congress men and women to support PNTR. Their effort in the Senate was easier in those days.

Talk that through. I mean, U.S. corporations send jobs to China, seem not to be on the side of human rights far too often in the workplace. U.S. policymakers seem to turn their heads oftentimes. Ms. Richardson speaks out that we treat China differently. I think this President has been more aggressive in trade enforcement than his three predecessors, but I think he has still fallen short.

The SED talks, the Strategic Economic Dialogue, never puts currency quite as front-and-center as I know a lot of us would like him to do. Or like our diplomats, our trade people, our finance, our treasury people to do—I'll read again Mr. Teng's comment that "countries like the United States often sacrifice human rights for trade with China." I will ask Dr. Richardson and Professor Clarke what they think of Mr. Teng's belief.

Mr. CLARKE. I think that in some cases that's true. I think the United States—for example, we recently heard that in Belgium during Xi Jinping's visit, and this also happened in London during Xi Jinping's visit, the police took extraordinary measures subsequently ruled illegal in the courts of that country to prevent Mr. Xi from the unpleasant site of Tibetan protests.

I think the United States is in the fortunate position of not having to make those compromises, and so if indeed U.S. trade officials or U.S. officials concerned with human rights are playing down their concerns for the benefits of trade with China, I think that's probably not necessary. I think China still needs the United States more than the United States needs China.

Chairman BROWN. Dr. Richardson?

Ms. RICHARDSON. I would agree with that. I do think that sometimes specific decisions or interventions are shelved as a result of trade, currency, or other economic issues, but I think human rights issues get subordinated for lots of different reasons, whether it's military, whether it's diplomatic, whether it's something at the Security Council.

I think one of the mistakes that gets made, partly because I think it is hard to do well, is to really integrate human rights issues across a much broader spectrum of different aspects of the bilateral relationship, but there is a lot of room and that's what Rice's remarks, I think, there quite good at in saying to different parts of the U.S. Government, this relationship is not going to fall apart if you raise this issue. You are actually in an unusually good position to press for a particular kind of change or a particular mistake.

I mean, if the larger question is about the relationship between China opening up economically and whether PNTR was a mistake, clearly raising income levels in China has been extremely beneficial in many ways. Obviously nobody is arguing against that. I think it's about both relating human rights issues to other issues in the bilateral relationship and not letting them fall victim, especially when they underpin them.

Chairman BROWN. Thank you, Dr. Richardson. Thanks.

Thank you again to Mr. Liu and the staff for their good work on this. I will turn it over to Congressman Walz and Congressman Pittenger to continue. Thanks to all four of you witnesses. We thank you very, very much.

Representative WALZ. Well, thank you. I just had a couple of follow-ups and then we'll see if Mr. Pittenger has anything on this. My question to each of you, and maybe our experts about this—about this a long time, as the United States re-sets its strategic position, if you will, we keep hearing about the re-set to the Pacific as the situations in the Middle East start to change and this re-set to the Pacific is both military, economic, supposedly much more geopolitical as we look at it.

How does this have an impact on this relationship? Does it change that? Does it bring more leverage or does it heighten the situation, because quite honestly, I think as we all know, there's going to be much more activity in the Pacific than there has been. So if anyone wants to try and grab that one.

Mr. CLARKE. Well, I guess China, or the Chinese Government, almost no matter what the United States does, is going to believe that the U.S. Government's speaking out about Chinese human rights is linked solely to U.S. strategic concerns, security concerns, and does not stem from a genuine concern on human rights, because they are going to look at their own report on human rights in the United States, which of course does not stem from concern about human rights in the United States but is simply a "so is your mother" response to the U.S. report on human rights in China.

So I think it's possible that the pivot to Asia could make China even more suspicious. It's certainly not going to make China less suspicious. It's probably going to make it more, but it's already at a very high level of suspicion and distrust about U.S. Government motives in this. So I think possibly for that reason it's important for the U.S. Government to support non-governmental initiatives in this area.

I think also—can I go back and answer your earlier question? I think it's important to realize there really are limits to what not just the United States, but anybody, can do. China is like a giant aircraft carrier and there are little rowboats tugging at it, trying to move the human rights situation in one way or the other. But what really is going to change the direction of that aircraft carrier is what is going on with the crew inside, and that's where real change is going to come from.

But as Dr. Richardson points out, legitimacy is very important. If you'll recall back when the Helsinki Accords were concluded, a lot of people thought, well, this is just giving the USSR the legitimacy it wants for its borders. And what did we get in return? A pig in a poke, this kind of commitment to human rights standards. But it turned out that that was very important. That sent an important signal to the internal dissident community in Russia and Eastern Europe.

So China is always going to act in its perceived interests, so if China thinks it's in its interests to cooperate with the United States over North Korean denuclearization, they're not going to stop doing it and go off in a hissy fit because some U.S. officials start raising human rights issues.

We often hear, "Oh, you know, the Chinese Government never responds to pressure." That's what the Chinese Government would like you to think, but of course it's nonsense. Why would anyone ever change the status quo until it starts getting unpleasant? So one has to make the status quo start getting unpleasant if one is going to have any hope of getting the Chinese Government to change its policies.

Ms. RICHARDSON. I'll just add a little bit of a different concern about the pivot Asia-wide. I can't improve on what Professor Clarke has just said, but simply to point out that the pivot does not appear to involve a commensurately greater effort on human rights issues in Asia.

In fact, it has been of serious concern to us that the pivot appears to have driven for, example, a desire to have much closer relations, for example, with countries like Vietnam, partly as a result of increased Chinese assertiveness or unproductive response to an increased U.S. presence. Vietnam has an appalling human rights record. It has led the United States to perhaps engage more in Indonesia, particularly with the military, than we think may be entirely appropriate. So it's hard to see the human rights dimension of the pivot itself.

Representative WALZ. Well, I'm fascinated by what—and all of you have said this, that we're looking—certainly trying to—you know, there is no magic bullet here and it's deep and it runs deep. But I think of these cultural changes.

I can still remember back to my China times in the 1980s and how shocked I was when I went into the social studies classroom and there was a picture of General Stillwell on the wall, that there was a group of Chinese who grew up in that time that saw things differently, and I guess maybe trying to cling to the hope that there's going to be cultural change and an understanding that we're in this together, as Dr. Teng pointed out, as constructively trying to get there, that we are proudly Chinese but we are also looking for some basic human rights issues.

I understand it's those deep-seated cultural changes that are the only things that are going to get at this. I'm trying to see, how do we foster those, whether it's—like what you're saying, is that pivot had better come with some other things than just forward bases in Guam, or whatever it ends up being.

Ms. RICHARDSON. Sorry, just one other quick point I'll add is that I don't know if we're using the word "culture" in the same way. I think it's about political power and who has access to it, and who has what rights and whether they're respected.

Representative WALZ. Yes.

Ms. RICHARDSON. But I think one other important dimension of the pivot and the New Citizens' Movement and sort of where we are at this time in history is to know that a number of the people, including those who are going to be tried or whose appeals are going to be heard this week, like Xu Zhiyong's, or people who I think sort of came of age politically in China in and around Tiananmen.

Representative WALZ. Yes.

Ms. RICHARDSON. We're bumping up against the 25th anniversary of that in a few months.

Representative WALZ. Yes.

Ms. RICHARDSON. It's extraordinary to think how little ground the Chinese Government has been willing to give on some of the same kinds of rights or freedoms that people were asking for in those circumstances. It's now the world's second-largest economy, it has an active space exploration program, and yet—and yet—25 years later Ding Zilin and the Tiananmen Mothers still can't get——

Representative WALZ. Yes, I think it's very insightful. Many of us mark time from that.

Ms. RICHARDSON. I do.

Representative WALZ. Yes, me too. Twenty years ago on June 4 I married my wife. There was no doubt I would remember that date. So, it's oddly enough how that works out.

But Mr. Pittenger, if you have any follow-up.

Representative PITTENGER. Thank you, Congressman Walz.

At the outset, Chairman Brown lamented that this is bipartisan or bicameral. I mean, we are all here and a large group of our congressional body, House and Senate, are truly committed to these concerns. Congressman Walz expressed his concerns as well.

I think I am reminded that 20 years ago I went to the former Soviet Union with Congressman Wolf—it was during Perestroika and Glasnost—and made our case for 119 dissidents imprisoned. We spent a week there. It was through an organization called Christian Solidarity but we were able to get these dissidents released from prison and have 3 million Bibles distributed because of the courage of a congressman and the courage of a member of Parliament, David Amess, who joined us on the trip.

I just wonder, I've been disappointed in the lack of commitment and voice by many administrations to speak to this issue when they had opportunity to do so, but what can we do as a Congress to speak out—and I don't know where this will take us, but I think we need to be more focused and clear and really think strategically on how this body can awaken this issue and bring it to the forefront. So thank you so much.

Ms. Ilham, I have four children, three of whom are daughters. You are a lovely lady, about the age of my daughters as well. I applaud you for your commitment, your love for your father, your commitment to him, your commitment to the freedom of other concerned like-minded people in China and your willingness to come forth today and to be with us. We are grateful for you and for your family.

Ms. ILHAM. Thank you so much.

Representative PITTENGER. God bless you.

Representative WALZ. Thanks, Mr. Pittenger.

I'd like to ask unanimous consent to submit Cochairman Representative Smith's statement for the record. No objection, so ordered.

I want to thank you all. We are grateful. We'll stay on this. You were right, Ms. Richardson, this is the best staff you could ever hope for. These are committed folks to getting it right. They're certainly a candle in the darkness at times and I appreciate that.

I think it's appropriate—before we adjourn, Ms. Ilham, you have earned the right to have the final word if you would like it.

Ms. ILHAM. Thank you so much for asking me to come here today to testify for my father, and thank you so much for all you have done for my father. Thank you so much.

Representative WALZ. With that, this Commission hearing is adjourned.

[The prepared statement of Representative Smith appears in the appendix.]

[Whereupon, at 4:50 p.m. the hearing was adjourned.]

APPENDIX

PREPARED STATEMENTS

PREPARED STATEMENT OF JEWHER ILHAM

APRIL 8, 2014

My name is Jewher Ilham and I am grateful to the Congressional-Executive Commission on China for giving me this opportunity to appear here and to speak to this committee about the suppression of dissent in the People's Republic of China as I have personally experienced it. I am currently enrolled as a student in the Intensive English Program at Indiana University and hope to matriculate into a degree program when I finish. This was not what I expected would happen to me over a year ago when I first set out to accompany my father, Ilham Tohti, to the U.S. where he was to take up a position as a visiting scholar at Indiana University in February, 2013. I was to stay for a month, helping my father set up his living arrangements; my father was to stay for a year.

My father, Ilham Tohti, is a well-known economist and writer based at Central Minzu University in Beijing, and an advocate for the human rights of the Uyghur people. Although I am Uyghur, I am not an academic expert on Xinjiang, nor an expert on Chinese politics. But I have been able to observe the impact and results of repressive Chinese policies as they have been applied to my father, his work, his students, and his family.

On February 2, 2013, after we arrived at the airport in Beijing and were checking in for our flight to the U.S., we were pulled out of line and taken away. When a bureaucratic error led to my being given the choice of continuing the boarding process and flying to the U.S. My father insisted that I continue the trip alone. He was detained, beaten, questioned and forbidden from leaving China. What were his crimes? On his website, *Uyghur Online,* and via other social media, he had written widely, about the abuses of basic human rights that are visited on the Uyghur people and that abridge their intellectual and religious freedoms. These policies, at their most egregious, leave them feeling like a people under occupation.

2013 was not the first time my father had been detained by the authorities, nor the first time that he and other members of our family had been subjected to harassment. The government was particularly enraged at the work my father did after serious clashes in Xinjiang in 2009 left many people dead and a significant number "disappeared." My father worked to get the names of these people out and to cast a spotlight on the lack of due process that was a large part of China's method of repressing Uyghur grievances. As a result of this work my family was removed from their residence and moved around for one month, our phones and computers confiscated.

This became familiar. In April 2011, my father and grandmother were sent to Guangzhou for a week. I stayed in Beijing with my mother (my parents are divorced). In December, I returned home from school one day and without forewarning found an empty home: my stepmother, my father and my brothers had been sent to Hainan for two weeks. On my own I made my way to my mother's home.

In 2012 the authorities the confiscated my five-year-old brother's residence book, thus blocking him from registering for school or having a passport. The university authorities also cancelled my father's classes for one semester without any explicit cause. Over the years too, *Uyghur Online* has been periodically shut down by the government.

In the fall of 2013 State Security personnel rammed my father's car when he was en route to the airport to pick up his mother, who was flying to Beijing from Urumqi. When he got out of his car the State Security people told him they would kill everyone in our family.

But the worst was what happened on and after January 15 of this year, the last day that any of our family saw my father. On that day 30 or 40 police from different offices came to our house and took my father away, confiscating documents, telephones, computers, and even our family safe. All this was done without any due process or requisite formalities. For days we had no information about his whereabouts; his lawyer was not allowed any contact with him. Then, on January 25, the Urumqi Public Security Bureau announced a slew of accusations against him, including inciting separatism and hatred of the country, as well as praising terrorists. Anyone who knows my father realizes how utterly false these charges are. One prominent Chinese intellectual has noted that my father is one of the few Uyghurs intellectuals and dissidents who, to his knowledge, does not favor separatism. My father never speaks about separatism; in fact he is exactly the sort of person a rational Chinese political structure would seek to engage with in order to address the conditions of the Uyghur people. Instead, by arresting my father and threatening him with charges that carry the severest of penalties it has driven many Uyghurs to a point at which they can't even imagine that their wholly justified grievances can get any sort of a hearing under Chinese rule. Today, we know that my father is being held in the Urumqi Municipal Prison. But no one can visit him.

The punishment of this honest, outspoken dissident doesn't stop here. The Chinese state doesn't just punish (justly or unjustly) an individual political prisoner. It often metes out a collective punishment to the prisoner's family. My stepmother has no access to family funds that legally belong to her because my father's bank account has been frozen. He has been the primary breadwinner for the family. She and my young brothers (ages 4 and 7) are monitored 24 hours a day by anywhere from 2–8 people; police sleep outside their door at night and keep watch there during the day.

Phone calls to my stepmother are monitored, making it difficult for her to communicate with me and with other people. In addition, the position that my stepmother has at Minzu University was always renewed periodically. But now we are seriously worried that when her current contract expires in May she may well lose her position due to my father's political imprisonment.

My brothers are also suffering gravely from this. The oldest, who is more aware than his brother as to what has happened, has become withdrawn and introverted. Having witnessed our father being taken away, he now has nightmares.

Finally, there are some students of my father. I am proud to say that my father was widely admired by his students, many of whom saw his work as vital and necessary. And now several of them too have been arrested and imprisoned, with very little known as to their whereabouts.

I mention these last facts to give you an idea of the kind of collective punishment that the arrest of dissidents entails. But the core matter here is that China has imprisoned a dissident intellectual whose sole "crime," in spite of the trumped up charges that are being thrown around, was simply advocating human rights and equitable treatment for the Uyghur people. I am heartened that the Congressional-Executive Commission on China has taken an interest in my father's case and is seeking to learn more about the facts of his imprisonment.

I thank you for allowing me to speak to you today.

PREPARED STATEMENT OF TENG BIAO

APRIL 8, 2014

I am a human rights lawyer from China. My name is Teng Biao.

In March, just before First Lady Michelle Obama gave a talk at the prestigious Peking University during her visit to China, I tweeted to draw her attention to the plight of two remarkable Peking University alumni: Cao Shunli and Xu Zhiyong.

On March 14, human rights activist Cao Shunli died in detention after being tortured and then denied medical treatment.

The last time I saw Ms. Cao was in Hong Kong at an international human rights workshop in early 2013. She had been released for the second time from detention in a *laojiaosuo,* a Reeducation Through Labor camp, and had immediately jumped back into the fray of defending human rights. In September last year the authorities at the Beijing International Airport where she was en route to Geneva to participate in the UN Human Rights Council Universal Periodic Review prevented Cao Shunli from leaving China. She was then abducted and detained for the third time, but this time, she did not come out alive.

For the past ten years, Dr. Xu Zhiyong has been one of the most prominent figures in the Chinese civil rights movement.

The last time I was in contact with him was a few days before he was formally arrested. He sent me a record of his conversation with the secret police. The government gave him several opportunities to compromise: if he agreed to abandon the New Citizens Movement he would be spared from incarceration. Dr. Xu refused outright to compromise.

He said, if fighting for citizen's rights and freedom is a crime, he was willing to pay the price. He prayed to God with these words: "I love mankind, and for this love I am willing to face death."

Dr. Xu was sentenced to four years in jail. He was charged with "disturbing public order" while publicly campaigning for equal rights of the children of migrant labours in cities, and demanding officials disclose assets in order to combat corruption. Several dozen supporters of Xu Zhiyong and the New Citizens Movement have been arrested and will soon be put on trial.

Incomplete statistics reveal that since March 31 last year, at least 200 rights advocates have been arrested, including human rights activists like Guo Feixiong, Zhang Lin, and Zhao Changqing who have been imprisoned numerous times for political reasons since 1989; rights lawyers like Ding Jiaxi; Zhang Shaojie, a pastor at a Christian Church in Henan province, and Ilham Tohti, a Uighur scholar who has been a long-time advocate of peaceful dialogue between Uighurs and Han Chinese.

It can be confirmed that during this crackdown, many human rights activists have been subjected to inhumane torture while incarcerated. People now released who were tortured include Ding Hongfen, Shen Jun, Song Ze; while Li Biyun, Huang Wenxun, Yuan Fengchu, Yuan Xiaohua, Liu Ping. Wei Zhongping, Li Sihua and others continue to be detained. All of these people were incarcerated for participating in peaceful and legal human rights activities. Five days after Cao Xunli died, the 43-year-old Tibetan political prisoner Goshul Lobsang was tortured to death in Kanlho.

To exacerbate the atmosphere of fear the authorities are targeting the family and friends of rights defenders: Liu Xia, the wife of Nobel Peace Prize laureate Liu Xiaobo has been under house arrest for many years; the families of many Tibetan self-immolators have been imprisoned, like 31 year-old Kunchok Wangmo of Ngaba (Chinese: Aba) Tibetan and Qiang Autonomous Prefecture, Sichuan, whose husband was framed for a crime and sentenced to death.

Many prisoners of conscience are connected to the New Citizens Movement. The earlier incarnation of the New Citizens Movement was a group called *Gongmeng*, or Open Constitution Initiative, founded by Xu Zhiyong and myself in 2003. The Open Constitution Initiative focussed on issues like freedom of speech, freedom of religious belief, opposition to torture, and opposition to the unfair household registration system. It actively joined in a large number of human rights cases such as those involving Gao Zhisheng and Chen Guangcheng, as well as producing an investigative report on the 14 March 2008 unrest in Tibet.

The New Citizens Movement advocates "Freedom, Justice and Love" to encourage ordinary people to fight for citizens rights and unite human rights advocates around the country. Its activities include: promoting educational equality, pressing officials to disclose their assets, and arranging "same-city dinner gathering". By using online mobilisation, open letter writing campaigns, signature campaigns, leaflet distribution, pro bono litigation, street speeches, and peaceful protests, The New Citizens Movement has brought the Rights Defence Movement to new heights.

Why is the Chinese government savagely suppressing the Rights Defence Movement and individual rights activists?

Since its inception in 2003, the Rights Defence Movement has made great progress. The earlier ground work of and the sacrifices made by activists, and the intensification of social conflicts reveal several trends: 1) Rights activists are coming out from cyberspace activism into real-world activism. 2) The movement is growing beyond individual cases to becoming active on the streets. 3) The activists are moving away from legal appeals towards political appeals. 4) Individual activists are gradually joining together creating a semblance of organisation. Examples are: Charter 08, the Chinese Human Rights Lawyers Group and the New Citizens Movement.

The authorities sense an obvious threat as the rights movement has progressed towards the New Citizens Movement. However, the rulers of China are unwilling to engage in dialogue and absolutely refuse to relinquish their totalitarian privileges. Under the guise of maintaining stability above all, the authorities brutally punish anyone who in their mind dares to threaten their legitimacy to rule China.

The government's heavy-handed crackdown will of course frighten some people, but cannot resolve social problems in Chinese society. On the contrary, suppression will only intensify conflicts and problems. Many rules and regulations in China directly violate people's dignity and freedom. The fissures in our society will become wider and calls for rights and democracy will become more intense if we do not make substantial adjustments to the country's legal and political systems. More and more people are standing up to demand rights and democracy.

For example, a few days ago, thousands of residents in Maoming, in Guangdong Province in southern China, risked their lives to take to the streets to protest plans for a paraxylene (PX) project which possess serious pollution risks.

Also recently, in Jiansanjiang in Heilongjiang Province in northern China, a number of lawyers were detained by local police for investigating a "Legal Education Center," informally known as a "brainwashing class," which is used to imprison innocent citizens without any legal procedure.

Three of these lawyers were roped and hung up while police punched and beat them with police batons.

Why did lawyers and citizens stand up and take on these "brainwashing classes"? Because they are modern-day concentration camps. Countless Falungong practitioners have been sent by the authorities to "brainwashing classes" or Re-education Through Labor camps. At least 3,000 people have been tortured to death in such places since 1999.

As a result of fighting for freedom, many human rights activists lose their own freedom. I recall the time in 2011 when the secret police in Beijing kidnapped me and held me in a secret location for 70 days, during which time I was subject to tortures including sleep deprivation, being punched and kicked, and being held in solitary confinement. While the secret police used violence against me, they frankly declared, "Don't talk to us about the law. No one can help you now."

But I never for a moment gave up hope. My longing for justice and freedom gave me strength. Another source of strength was my firm belief that my friends in jail and on the outside would continue to fight, because we share the same dream for freedom. I firmly believe that our numbers will grow and that our calls for freedom will ultimately stun this savage totalitarian regime to its core.

I also firmly believe that outside China, in the USA, in Europe and in every corner of the world where the light of freedom shines, while the struggle for human dignity continues, we will not be forgotten.

I greatly admire the members of Congress and the American government for your efforts in advocating freedom and human rights. However, the international pressure on violators of human rights around the world is far from adequate. The Chinese government not only manipulates the international human rights system, it also makes use of its economic, military and political influence in order to blackmail great democratic nations. It threatens not to purchase Boeing jets if America criticises the Chinese human rights situation. It threatens not to purchase Airbuses if European leaders meet with the Dalai Lama. At many international conferences Chinese human rights has become "the elephant in the room".

How much economic benefit can we sacrifice for the freedom of humanity? When people make this calculation, they are already on the wrong track. Oppressors of freedom will not desist, they will not respect national boundaries, they will not abide by international principles they have promised to follow.

The oppressors of freedom are becoming more powerful by taking advantage of the internet and economic globalisation, by taking advantage of flawed international institutions (the most egregious violators of human rights have colluded to infiltrate the UN Human Rights Commission, and non-democratic regimes in the UN are betraying the interests of their own peoples as well as universal human rights), by taking advantage of the head-in-the-sand policies of democratic countries and "the silence of the good". By the time the free world becomes aware of the need to protect freedom, I fear it may well be too late.

————

PREPARED STATEMENT OF DONALD CLARKE*

The Significance of Recent Detentions for the Rule of Law in China

APRIL 8, 2014

Introduction

In my testimony today, I will look at two recent detentions in China and discuss their significance for the rule of law in China. The detentions are those of Xu Zhiyong and Ilham Tohti. I believe that the main significance of these detentions lies not in the substance of the charges against them or the sentences, but rather in the process that accompanied the detentions. It is not news that the Chinese government persecutes those it deems its enemies, so these cases aren't especially significant in that respect. But unlike in some other cases, in these cases the Chinese government has for the most part acted in such a way that it is hard to find clear and unambiguous violations of Chinese procedural rules. Whether it has done so depends on the interpretation of vague concepts such as whether a case is "complex".

Thus, while the rule of law has no place in the investigation and prosecution of Bo Xilai and now Zhou Yongkang, both of whom were and are respectively detained under a Party disciplinary procedure that in legal terms amounts to the crime of unlawful detention, it seems that the authorities are paying more attention to following their own rules in other cases. But those rules are so vague and elastic that even when followed, they offer little protection to defendants. While "rule of law" is an appealing slogan because it seems to command such broad adherence, it does so precisely because it does not necessarily dictate substantively just results. It is better than no rule of law, as Bo Xilai might now ruefully admit. But it is not synonymous with the protection of human rights. It is a necessary but not a sufficient condition.

Xu Zhiyong

Xu Zhiyong's current troubles began when he was placed under an informal kind of "house arrest" on April 12, 2013. This meant that he was effectively a prisoner in his own home. I call this kind of detention "informal" because while Chinese law has a form of house arrest called "residential surveillance," it's not clear that that procedure was specifically invoked.

His formal detention began on July 16, 2013.[1] That date is important because itunambiguously started the clock in China's Criminal Procedure Law (CPL) ticking. Detention (*juliu*) in China is a different concept from arrest (*daibu*); whereas in the United States we use the term "arrest" to refer to any situation in which a suspect is not free to leave, the same English word in the Chinese context is used to translate a formal stage of the criminal process that can happen long after a suspect has been locked up.

Detention without arrest is supposed to happen only in a limited set of essentially emergency circumstances (CPL 61); where those emergency circumstances are not present, the police are supposed to get approval for an arrest before physically detaining the suspect. In Xu's case, it is fair to say that none of those emergency circumstances existed.

After detention, the police have three days, extendable to seven days in special circumstances, to request the approval of arrest by the procuracy, the body in charge of prosecutions. In complex cases involving, for example, multiple offenses, the period can be as long as thirty days (CPL 89). The procuracy has seven days in which to decide to approve or disapprove the arrest. In Xu's case, the indictment says he was formally arrested on August 22, 2014.[2] This is exactly thirty days plus seven days following hisformal detention; apparently someone in charge was keeping a close eye on the calendar. To call this arrest lawful, however, we would have to be satisfied that the term during which he was under house arrest prior to his formal detention was lawful.

The closest thing China has to house arrest is an institution called "supervised residence" (*jianshi juzhu*) (CPL 72). This is the only lawful rubric under which Xu could have been confined to his residence as he was prior to his formal detention. But supervised residence requires, among other conditions that arguably were not present here, that the conditions for arrest *already be deemed met*. In that case, it is impossible to justify under Chinese law Xu's subsequent 37 days in formal detention prior to his arrest, since the authorities must have decided he was arrestable as early as April 12.David A. Weaver Research Professor of Law, George Washington University Law School, dclarke@law.gwu.edu. I wish to thank Fu Hualing and Joshua Rosenzweig for very helpful comments on an earlier draft.

Xu was arrested on a charge of "gathering crowds to disrupt order in a public place" (Criminal Law 291). Once a suspect is arrested, the authorities have two months—extendable to three with appropriate permission—to keep him in custody while they investigate (CPL 154). This time limit can be extended two months by provincial authorities in complex cases (CPL 156). Even this five-month time limit can be extended indefinitely by action of the Standing Committee of the National People's Congress (CPL 155).

Thus, he should have been released or put on trial by October 22, 2013, unless certain very unusual circumstances applied to his case. But Xu was not put on trial until January 22, 2014, exactly five months after his formal arrest. This suggests that the generous time limits afforded by Articles 154 and 156 of the CPL were used to the full—something that should hardly have been necessary, given the Foreign Ministry's insistence that Xu's was "an ordinary criminal case."[3]

The excessive period of pre-arrest custody was not the only flaw in the proceedings. The trial itself was marred by numerous violations of the letter and spirit of Chinese law. First, the trial was not in any real sense open, despite the lack of any grounds under Chinese law for closing it. Second, the defense was not permitted to cross-examine any witnesses for the prosecution, despite the rule providing for cross-examination or at least some way to challenge evidence in the CPL. It should

---

[1] *See China Detains Activist Xu Zhiyong*, BBC NEWS, July 17, 2013, http://bbc.in/1mV3zEA.
[2] The indictment is available in English translation at *Xu Zhiyong's Indictment* http://www.hrichina.org/en/citizens-square/xu-zhiyongs-indictment.
[3] *See* Jerome Cohen, *Xu Zhiyong's Trial Makes a Mockery of Beijing's Pledge to Enforce Rule of Law,* SOUTH CHINA MORNING POST, Jan. 29, 2014, available at http://bit.ly/MjWYE5.

be noted that Xu's case is not unique in that regard; the CPL's rule is honored far more in the breach than in the observance. Third, Xu was not permitted to call his own witnesses.[4]

To protest these and other problems, Xu and his counsel elected to remain silent during the hearing. At the end, Xu attempted to make a statement, but was cut off by the judge.[5] In the end, he was sentenced to four years of imprisonment.

Ilham Tohti

Ilham Tohti was detained on Jan. 15, 2014.[6] He was apparently formally arrested on Feb. 20, 2014 on a charge of separatism (*fenlie guojia*).[7] This period of time between detention and arrest could fit within that allowed under Chinese law[8] if his case is complex. So far, the time between arrest and trial has not been exceeded; the authorities are well within the permitted time period.

Nevertheless, the state has deprived Tohti of his rights under Chinese law in other ways. On March 4, 2014, his lawyer, Li Fangping, stated that he was no longer allowed to communicate with Tohti.[9] Apparently the reason given was that state secrets wereinvolved. Unfortunately, the Chinese government has used this excuse so often in circumstances where it is highly implausible that it no longer carries any credibility. Occasionally the police have claimed that conditions of detention and interrogation are themselves state secrets, but if this is to constitute a reason for depriving defendants of their right to communicate with a lawyer, then the right is meaningless for all suspects in detention.

Analysis

The point of this detailed history of the Xu and Tohti cases is not to condemn the Chinese government for violating its own rules. It is to further our understanding of the significance of these cases for the rule of law in China.

There are two lessons here. First, following legal procedures is better than not following legal procedures, but it does not necessarily produce justice. We have to ask what the laws say and how they were produced. In Chinese criminal procedure, the rules are heavily weighted in favor of the state, and there is no neutral process to challenge the state's interpretation in its own favor of vague and ambiguous concepts.

The second lesson is that the Chinese government retains its ambivalent attitude toward the values of the rule of law. As I have noted, in many cases the government wishes to claim the mantle of fidelity to law; it does so sometimes by making the law vague and flexible enough to achieve its purposes, and sometimes simply by falsely claiming to be following law. One can call this hypocrisy, but hypocrisy is after all the compliment that vice pays to virtue, and it reflects an acknowledgment of the value of process protections.

At other times, however, the state does not seem to be trying even to *appear* to offer fair proceedings, or at least proceedings that follow its own rules. This is what we see in the trial proceedings of Xu Zhiyong and will probably see in Ilham Tohti's trial. While other authoritarian states often try to turn political issues into legal issues in an attempt to neutralize them,[10] the Chinese state sometimes seems to go out of its way to demonstrate that ostensibly legal issues are really political

---

[4] *See* Andrew Jacobs & Chris Buckley, *China Sentences Xu Zhiyong, Legal Activist, to 4 Years in Prison*, N.Y. TIMES, Jan. 26, 2014, available at http://nyti.ms/1hQDL98.

[5] *See id.*

[6] *See China: Uighur Scholar Detained*, N.Y. TIMES, Jan. 16, 2014, *available at* http://nyti.ms/PBBXXp.

[7] *See* Bei Feng, *Yilihamu Tuheti Bei Daibu* [Ilham Tohti Arrested], Feb. 25, 2014, http://canyu.org/n85273c6.aspx. This source reproduces what purports to be a notice issued to Tohti's spouse. The notice is dated Feb. 20, 2014.

The crime of separatism is listed in the first paragraph of Art. 103 of the Criminal Law. The second paragraph lists a lesser crime of "inciting separatism" (*shandong fenlie guojia*). Under Art. 113 of the Criminal Law, separatism, but not inciting separatism, is punishable in some circumstances by death. The *New York Times* reported that Tohti was formally arrested on Feb. 26 and charged with "inciting separatism," *see* Andrew Jacobs, *China Charges Scholar with Inciting Separatism*, N.Y. TIMES, Feb. 26, 2014, *available at* http://nyti.ms/1hli1lg, but Bei Feng, *supra*, unless the document it purports to cite is spurious, contradicts this.

[8] Chinese law allows a 24-hour period of "summons" before formal detention, then up to thirty days before the police must request an arrest, and then seven days for the procuratorate to make a decision, for a total of 38 days following actual detention.

[9] *See* Massoud Hayoun, *China, Uyghurs May Have Lost Middle Way in Mounting Ethnic Tensions*, AL JAZEERA AMERICA, Mar. 4, 2014, http://alj.am/1ejnipp.

[10] *See generally* RULE BY LAW: THE POLITICS OF COURTS IN AUTHORITARIAN REGIMES (Tom Ginsburg & Tamir Moustafa eds. 2008).

issues. Thus, it is really not clear whether it is reasonable to expect at least a slow movement toward the values of process.

Perhaps equally significant for prospects for a process-oriented rule of law in China is the fact that the government's indifference to the values of process seems to be shared by at least some of its critics. Recently five Chinese legal scholars were brave enough to post a public analysis of the flaws in the case against Xu Zhiyong.[11] Yet their analysisconsisted entirely of a defense of Xu against the substance of the charges made against him. They argued that he had not actually created a disturbance of public order, or that the public spaces in question were special. These kinds of arguments might be useful in a court before a neutral judge, but since they are basically expressions of opinion about what the law means or ought to mean, they lack force. The scholars made no objections to any of the procedural problems in the case. As I have pointed out, the pre-trial procedural flaws are not clear-cut. But they are certainly not harder to criticize than the substantive charges, so it is unfortunate that this critique ignored procedural problems both before and during the trial.

One advantage of a procedural critique is that the government can be criticized without ever questioning the validity of its stated laws and policies. Thus, it is ironic that even the government's critics may share its view that it is the substance of the law that counts, not procedure, even though the best way to advance the rule of law in the current political climate might be to focus on procedure.

* David A. Weaver Research Professor of Law, George Washington University Law School, dclarke@law.gwu.edu. I wish to thank Fu Hualing and Joshua Rosenzweig for very helpful comments on an earlier draft.

————

PREPARED STATEMENT OF SOPHIE RICHARDSON

APRIL 8, 2014

Rapid socio-economic change in China has been accompanied by relaxation of some restrictions on basic rights, but the government remains an authoritarian one-party state. It places arbitrary curbs on expression, association, assembly, and religion; prohibits independent labor unions and human rights organizations; and maintains Party control over all judicial institutions.

The government censors the press, the Internet, print publications, and academic research, and justifies human rights abuses as necessary to preserve "social stability." It carries out involuntary population relocation and rehousing on a massive scale, and enforces highly repressive policies in ethnic minority areas in Tibet, Xinjiang, and Inner Mongolia. Though primary school enrollment and basic literacy rates are high, China's education system discriminates against children and young people with disabilities. The government obstructs domestic and international scrutiny of its human rights record, insisting it is an attempt to destabilize the country.

At the same time, citizens are increasingly prepared to challenge authorities over volatile livelihood issues, such as land seizures, forced evictions, environmental degradation, miscarriages of justice, abuse of power by corrupt cadres, discrimination, and economic inequality. Official and scholarly statistics, based on law enforcement reports, suggest there are 300–500 protests each day, with anywhere from ten to tens of thousands of participants. Despite the risks, Internet users and reform-oriented media are aggressively pushing censorship boundaries by advocating for the rule of law and transparency, exposing official wrongdoing, and calling for political reforms.

Civil society groups and advocates continue to slowly expand their work despite their precarious status, and an informal but resilient network of activists monitors and documents human rights cases as a loose national "weiquan" (rights defense) movement. These activists endure police monitoring, detention, arrest, enforced disappearance, and torture.

The Xi Jinping administration formally assumed power in March, and proposed several reforms to longstanding policies, including abolishing one form of arbitrary detention, known as re-education through labor (RTL), and changes to the household registration system. It staged high-profile corruption investigations, mostly targeting political rivals. But it also struck a conservative tone, opposing constitutional rule, press freedom, and "western-style" rule of law, and issuing harsher restrictions

————

[11] See Gan Peizhong Deng Wuwei Faxue Jiaoshou Fabiao Lunzheng Xu Zhiyong Wuzui de Falü Yijian Shu [Gan Peizhong and Four Other Law Professors Issue Legal Opinion Arguing that Xu Zhiyong Is Innocent], BOXUN.COM, Jan. 27, 2014, http://bit.ly/1kAgVBR (presenting text of letter issued by Gan Peizhong, Peng Bing, Yao Huanqing, Wang Yong, and He Haibo).

on dissent, including through two legal documents making it easier to bring criminal charges against activists and Internet critics.

Bo Xilai, once a rising political star, was sentenced to life imprisonment in September after a show trial that captured public attention but fell short of fair trial standards and failed to address widespread abuses of power committed during his tenure in Chongqing.

Human Rights Defenders

China's human rights activists often face imprisonment, detention, torture, commitment to psychiatric facilities, house arrest, and intimidation.

One of the most severe crackdowns on these individuals in recent years occurred in 2013, with more than 50 activists put under criminal detention between February and October. Human rights defenders are detained for ill-defined crimes ranging from "creating disturbances" to "inciting subversion" for organizing and participating in public, collective actions. In July, authorities detained Xu Zhiyong, who is considered an intellectual leader of the New Citizens Movement, a loose network of civil rights activists whose efforts include a nationwide campaign that calls on public officials to disclose their assets.

In September, Beijing-based activist Cao Shunli was detained after she was barred from boarding a flight to Geneva ahead of the United Nations Human Rights Council (HRC) review of China on October 22. Cao is known for pressing the Chinese government to include independent civil society input into the drafting of China's report to the HRC under a mechanism called Universal Periodic Review (UPR). Another activist, Peng Lanlan, was released in August after she spent one year in prison for "obstructing official business" for her role in the campaign.

Nobel Peace Prize winner Liu Xiaobo continues his 11-year jail term in northern Liaoning province. His wife Liu Xia continues to be subjected to unlawful house arrest. In August, Liu Xiaobo's brother-in-law, Liu Hui, was given an 11-year sentence on fraud charges; it is widely believed the heavy sentence is part of broader effort to punish Liu Xiaobo's family.

Legal Reforms

While the government rejects judicial independence and prohibits independent bar associations, progressive lawyers and legal scholars continue to be a force for change, contributing to increasing popular legal awareness and activism.

The Chinese Communist Party maintains authority over all judicial institutions and coordinates the judiciary's work through its political and legal committees. The Public Security Bureau, or police, remains the most powerful actor in the criminal justice system. Use of torture to extract confessions is prevalent, and miscarriages of justice are frequent due to weak courts and tight limits on the rights of the defense.

In November, the government announced its intention to abolish re-education through labor (RTL), a form of arbitrary detention in which the police can detain people for up to four years without trial. There were about 160,000 people in about 350 camps at the beginning of the year, but numbers dwindled rapidly as the police stopped sending people to RTL. The official press, however, reported that some of these facilities were being converted to drug rehabilitation centers, another form of administrative detention. At time of writing it was unclear whether the government would fully abolish administrative detention as a way to deal with minor offenders, or whether it would instead establish a replacement system that continued to allow detention without trial.

China continues to lead the world in executions. The exact number remains a state secret, but experts estimate it has decreased progressively from about 10,000 per year a decade ago to less than 4,000 in recent years.

Freedom of Expression

Freedom of expression deteriorated in 2013, especially after the government launched a concerted effort to rein in micro-blogging. The government and the Party maintain multiple layers of control over all media and publications.

Internet censors shape online debate and maintain the "Great Firewall," which blocks outside content from reaching Internet users in China. Despite these restrictions, the Internet, especially microblog services known as "weibo" and other social media tools, are popular as a relatively free space in which China's 538 million users can connect and air grievances. However, those who breach sensitive taboos are often swiftly identified and their speech deleted or disallowed; some are detained or jailed.

In January, *Southern Weekly,* a Guangzhou-based newspaper known for its boundary-pushing investigative journalism, was enveloped in a censorship row after the paper's editors found that their New Year's special editorial was rewritten on the censors' orders and published without their consent. The original editorial had called for political reform and respect for constitutionally guaranteed rights, but the published version instead praised the Chinese Communist Party. The

paper's staff publicly criticized the provincial top censor, called for his resignation and went on a strike; the paper resumed printing a week later.

In May, the General Office of the Chinese Communist Party's Central Committee issued a gag order to universities directing them to avoid discussions of "seven taboos," which included "universal values" and the Party's past wrongs, according to media reports.

Since August, authorities have waged a campaign against "online rumors." The campaign has targeted influential online opinion leaders and ordinary netizens. The authorities have detained hundreds of Internet users for days, closed down over 100 "illegal" news websites run by citizen journalists, and detained well-known liberal online commentator Charles Xue.

Also in August, the government official in charge of Internet affairs warned Internet users against breaching "seven bottom lines," including China's "socialist system," the country's "national interests," and "public order." In September, the Supreme People's Court and the Supreme People's Procuratorate (state prosecutor) issued a new judicial interpretation applying four existing criminal provisions to Internet expression, providing a more explicit legal basis for charging Internet users.

Freedom of Religion

Although the constitution guarantees freedom of religion, the government restricts religious practices to officially approved mosques, churches, temples, and monasteries organized by five officially recognized religious organizations. It audits the activities, employee details, and financial records of religious bodies, and retains control over religious personnel appointments, publications, and seminary applications.

Unregistered spiritual groups such as Protestant "house churches" are deemed unlawful and subjected to raids and closures; members are harassed and leaders are detained and sometimes jailed.

The government classifies Falun Gong, a meditation-focused spiritual group banned since July 1999, as an "an evil cult" and arrests, harasses, and intimidates its members. After releasing a new documentary about a labor camp in which Falun Gong practitioners were detained and tortured, filmmaker and photographer Du Bin was detained in May. He was released after five weeks in detention.

In April, a court in Henan province sentenced seven house church leaders to between three and seven years in prison on charges of "using a cult to undermine law enforcement" evidence suggested they had only attended meetings and publicized church activities.

Health and Disability Rights

The government has developed numerous laws, regulations, and action plans designed to decrease serious environmental pollution and related threats to public health, but the policies are often not implemented.

In February, a lawyer's request under the Open Government Information Act to reveal soil contamination data was rejected; according to the authorities, such data was a "state secret." Also in February, after years of denial and inaction, the Ministry of Environmental Protection finally acknowledged the existence of "cancer villages," those with abnormally high cancer rates. Victims had long pressed for justice and compensation and domestic media had written extensively on the issue.

Despite a review in 2012 under the Convention on the Rights of Persons with Disabilities (CRPD), protections of the rights of persons with disabilities remain inadequate. These individuals face serious discrimination in employment and education, and some government policies institutionalize discrimination.

In February, the State Council's Legislative Affairs Office announced amendments to the 1994 Regulations of Education of Persons with Disabilities in China. While welcome, the amendments do not ensure that students with disabilities can enroll in mainstream schools or mandate appropriate classroom modifications ("accommodations") enabling them to participate fully in such schools.

In May, China's first Mental Health Law came into effect. It filled an important legal void but does not close loopholes that allow government authorities and families to detain people in psychiatric hospitals against their will. In July, after the law came into effect, Gu Xianghong was detained for five weeks in a Beijing psychiatric hospital for petitioning the authorities about her grievances.

Women's Rights

Women's reproductive rights and access to reproductive health remain severely curtailed under China's population planning regulations. While the government announced in November that Chinese couples will now be allowed two children if either parent was a single child, the measure does not change the foundations of China's government-enforced family planning policy, which includes the use of legal and other coercive measures—such as administrative sanctions, fines, and coercive measures, including forced abortion—to control reproductive choices.

The government's punitive crackdowns on sex work often lead to serious abuses, including physical and sexual violence, increased risk of disease, and constrained access to justice for the country's estimated 4 to 10 million sex workers, most of whom are women. Sex workers have also documented abuses by public health agencies, such as coercive HIV testing, privacy infringements, and mistreatment by health officials.

In January, the Supreme People's Court upheld a death sentence against Li Yan, a woman convicted of murdering her physically abusive husband. Domestic violence is not treated as a mitigating factor in court cases.

In May, Ye Haiyan, China's most prominent sex worker rights activist, was detained by police for several days after being assaulted at her home in Guangxi province over her exposure of abusive conditions in local brothels.

Although the government acknowledges that domestic violence, employment discrimination, and gender bias are widespread, it limits the activities of independent women's rights groups working on these issues by making it difficult for them to register, monitoring their activities, interrogating their staff, and prohibiting some activities.

Migrant and Labor Rights

The official All-China Federation of Trade Unions (ACFTU) continued to be the only legal representative of workers; independent labor unions are forbidden.

Despite this limitation, workers have become increasingly vocal and active in striving for better working conditions across the country, including by staging protests and strikes. In September, Shenzhen dock workers went on strike to demand better pay and working conditions. Ten days later, the workers accepted a government-brokered deal that met some of their demands.

In May, the official All-China Women's Federation issued a new report revealing that the number of migrant children, including those living with their parents in urban areas and those "left behind" in rural areas, had reached 100 million by 2010. Migrant workers continue to be denied urban residence permits, which are required to gain access to social services such as education. Many such workers leave their children at home when they migrate so that the children can go to school, rendering some vulnerable to abuse.

Although China has numerous workplace safety regulations, enforcement is lax, especially at the local level. For example, in June, a fire at a poultry farm killed 121 workers in Jilin province. Subsequent investigations revealed that the local fire department had just days before the fire issued the poultry farm a safety certificate even though it failed to meet a number of standards.

Sexual Orientation and Gender Identity

The Chinese government classified homosexuality as a mental illness until 2001. To date there is still no law protecting people from discrimination on the basis of sexual orientation or gender identity, which remains common especially in the workplace.

Same-sex partnership and marriage are not recognized under Chinese law. In February, a lesbian couple attempted to register at the marriage registry in Beijing but their application was rejected.

On May 17, the International Day against Homophobia, Changsha city authorities detained Xiang Xiaohan, an organizer of a local gay pride parade, and held him for 12 days for organizing an "illegal march." In China, demonstrations require prior permission, which is rarely granted.

Tibet

The Chinese government systematically suppresses political, cultural, religious and socio-economic rights in Tibet in the name of combating what it sees as separatist sentiment. This includes nonviolent advocacy for Tibetan independence, the Dalai Lama's return, and opposition to government policy. At time of writing, 123 Tibetans had self-immolated in protest against Chinese policies since the first recorded case in February 2009.

Arbitrary arrest and imprisonment remains common, and torture and ill-treatment in detention is endemic. Fair trials are precluded by a politicized judiciary overtly tasked with suppressing separatism.

Police systematically suppress any unauthorized gathering. On July 6, police opened fire in Nyitso, Dawu prefecture (Ch. Daofu), on a crowd that had gathered in the countryside to celebrate the Dalai Lama's birthday. Several people were injured. The government censored news of the event.

In an apparent effort to prevent a repetition of the popular protests of 2008, the government in 2013 maintained many of the measures it introduced during its brutal crackdown on the protest movement—a massive security presence composed largely of armed police forces, sharp restrictions on the movements of Tibetans within the Tibetan plateau, increased controls on monasteries, and a ban on foreign journalists in the Tibetan Autonomous Region (TAR) unless part of a government-organized tour. The government also took significant steps to implement a plan to station 20,000 new officials and Party cadres in the TAR, including in every village, to monitor the political views of all residents.

The government is also subjecting millions of Tibetans to a mass rehousing and relocation policy that radically changes their way of life and livelihoods, in some cases impoverishing them or making them dependent on state subsidies, about which they have no say. Since 2006, over two million Tibetans, both farmers and herders, have been involuntarily "rehoused"—through government-ordered renovation or construction of new houses—in the TAR; hundreds of thousands of nomadic herders in the eastern part of the Tibetan plateau have been relocated or settled in "New Socialist Villages."

Xinjiang

Pervasive ethnic discrimination, severe religious repression, and increasing cultural suppression justified by the government in the name of the "fight against separatism, religious extremism, and terrorism" continue to fuel rising tensions in the Xinjiang Uyghur Autonomous Region.

In 2013, over one hundred people—Uyghurs, Han, and other ethnicities—were killed in various incidents across the region, the highest death toll since the July 2009 Urumqi protests. In some cases, heavy casualties appear to have been the result of military-style assaults on groups preparing violent attacks, as in Bachu prefecture on April 23, and in Turfan prefecture on June 26. But in other cases security forces appear to have used lethal force against crowds of unarmed protesters.

On June 28, in Hetian prefecture, police tried to prevent protesters from marching toward Hetian municipality to protest the arbitrary closure of a mosque and the arrest of its imam, ultimately shooting into the crowd and injuring dozens of protesters. On August 8, in Aksu prefecture, police forces prevented villagers from reaching a nearby mosque to celebrate a religious festival, eventually using live ammunition and injuring numerous villagers. After each reported incident the government ritualistically blames "separatist, religious extremist, and terrorist forces," and obstructs independent investigations.

Arbitrary arrest, torture, and "disappearance" of those deemed separatists are endemic and instill palpable fear in the population. In July, Ilham Tohti, a Uyghur professor at Beijing's Nationalities University published an open letter to the government asking for an investigation into 34 disappearance cases he documented. Tohti was placed under house arrest several times and prevented from traveling abroad.

The government continues to raze traditional Uyghur neighborhoods and rehouse families in planned settlements as part of a comprehensive development policy launched in 2010. The government says the policy is designed to urbanize and develop Xinjiang.

Hong Kong

Despite the fact that Hong Kong continues to enjoy an independent judiciary, a free press, and a vocal civil society, freedoms of the press and assembly have been increasingly under threat since Hong Kong returned to Chinese sovereignty in 1997. Prospects that election of the territory's chief executive starting in 2017 would be genuinely competitive dimmed after Beijing indicated that only candidates who did not "oppose the central government" would be able to run.

Hong Kong has witnessed slow erosion of the rule of law in recent years, exemplified by increasingly strict police controls on assemblies and processions, and arbitrary Immigration Department bans on individuals critical of Beijing, such as members of the Falun Gong and exiled dissidents from the 1989 democracy spring.

Chinese Foreign Policy

Despite China's continued rise as a global power and its 2013 leadership transition, including the appointment of a new foreign minister, long-established foreign policy views and practices remained relatively unchanged.

China has become more engaged with various United Nations mechanisms but has not significantly improved its compliance with international human rights standards or pushed for improved human rights protections in other countries. In a notable exception, shortly after it was elected to the UN Human Rights Council in November, China publicly urged Sri Lanka "to make efforts to protect and promote human rights."

Even in the face of the rapidly growing death toll in Syria and evidence in August 2013 that the Syrian government used chemical weapons against civilians, Beijing has continued to object to any significant Security Council measures to increase pressure on the Assad regime and abusive rebel groups. It has opposed referral of the situation to the International Criminal Court (ICC) and an arms embargo against forces that commit widespread human rights or laws of war violations. China has also slowed down Security Council-driven efforts to deliver desperately needed humanitarian assistance across the border to rebel controlled areas in northern Syria.

In a minor change of tactics, if not of longer-term strategy, Chinese authorities have become modestly more vocal in their public and private criticisms of North Korea, particularly following actions by Pyongyang that increased tensions between members of the six-party talks aimed at addressing security concerns posed by North Korea's nuclear weapons program.

Both private and state-owned Chinese firms continue to be a leading source of foreign direct investment, particularly in developing countries, but in some cases have been unwilling or unable to comply with international labor standards.

Key International Actors

Most governments that have bilateral human rights dialogues with the Chinese government, including the United States, European Union, and Australia, held at least one round of those dialogues in 2013; most acknowledge they are of limited utility for promoting meaningful change inside China.

Several of these governments publicly expressed concern about individual cases, such as those of Xu Zhiyong or Liu Hui, or about trends such as restrictions on anti-corruption activists. Ambassadors from the US and Australia, as well as the EU's special representative for human tights, were allowed to visit the TAR or other Tibetan areas.

None of these governments commented on the denial of Chinese people's political rights to choose their leaders during the 2012–2013 leadership transition, and few successfully integrated human rights concerns into meetings with senior Chinese officials.

China participated in a review of its compliance with the Convention on the Rights of Persons with Disabilities by the international treaty body charged with monitoring implementation of the convention and a review of its overall human rights record at the UN Human Rights Council, but it failed to provide basic information or provided deeply misleading information on torture, arbitrary detention, and restrictions on freedom of expression. There are eight outstanding requests to visit China by UN special rapporteurs, and UN agencies operating inside China remain tightly restricted, their activities closely monitored by the authorities.

PREPARED STATEMENT OF HON. SHERROD BROWN, A U.S. SENATOR FROM OHIO; CHAIRMAN, CONGRESSIONAL-EXECUTIVE COMMISSION ON CHINA

APRIL 8, 2014

On February 21, nine Members of this Commission—Democrats and Republicans from both the House and the Senate—sent a letter to Chinese President Xi Jinping, urging him to end the crackdown on rights advocates in China.

Among the cases we highlighted was that of Uyghur scholar Ilham Tohti, and his daughter joins us today. Mr. Tohti is a thoughtful and peaceful advocate of the rights of the Uyghur minority, who has sought to build bridges among ethnic groups. We are grateful that his daughter joined us today.

We are grateful that the prominent human rights lawyer Teng Biao could join us via Skype. Teng Biao has provided legal assistance in human rights cases at great risk to himself. Our staff has made every effort to ensure the security of this feed and we hope there will be no disruption.

We are grateful, too, that Mr. Clarke and Ms. Richardson could take time out of their busy schedules to be here. Ms. Richardson is a respected expert on human rights. Mr. Clarke has done considerable research into understanding China's legal reform and rule of law development.

This hearing comes at an important time.

President Xi Jinping has been in power more than a year.

As we will learn more today, he has presided over a worrisome crackdown that is estimated to have swept away more than 150 activists, lawyers, journalists, and intellectuals.

President Xi spoke of respecting the Constitution and rule of law when he entered office. He has talked tough on corruption. His government has pledged to protect ethnic minorities.

But when his own citizens, including the father of our witness today, sought to hold the Chinese government accountable they were punished.

They include the legal advocate Xu Zhiyong, who has sought to promote educational opportunity and transparency of officials' finances. He is now serving a four-year sentence for "disturbing social order."

They include the activist Cao Shunli, who sought to participate in the drafting of China's human rights report to be presented to the UN Human Rights Council. She died last month after being detained and denied medical treatment.

They include the four lawyers trying to defend Falun Gong members held in illegal detention centers known as black jails. The lawyers have been detained and beaten.

During President Xi's first year in office we have learned that independent voices—even those that echo the government's concerns and try to uphold the law—will not be tolerated.

These actions are not befitting a country that every day claims to want, and is seeking, in fact, greater international legitimacy.

We urge the government of the People's Republic of China to respect the fundamental rights of every one of its citizens to freedom of expression, press, association, and religion.

We do so not simply because this is China's obligation under international law, but because China will be better and stronger if it gives its citizens a voice and stake in the system.

By listening to and respecting the rights of citizens like Ilham Tohti and Xu Zhiyong, China can involve all its people in dealing with the most important problems of the day—corruption, ethnic tensions, income inequality.

But first, President Xi and China's leaders must view these citizens not as threats but as people who want what's best for their country.

I look forward to hearing the witnesses.

————

PREPARED STATEMENT OF HON. CHRISTOPHER SMITH, A U.S. REPRESENTATIVE FROM NEW JERSEY; COCHAIRMAN, CONGRESSIONAL-EXECUTIVE COMMISSION ON CHINA

APRIL 8, 2014

On the morning of March 14th, Cao Shunli died alone at Beijing Military Hospital #309. Chinese police detained her on September 14, 2013, after she attempted to attend the UN Human Rights Council's review of China's human rights record.

She was officially detained on the bogus charge of "suspicion of illegal assembly" and "creating a disturbance." During her six month detention she was repeatedly denied medical care for serious conditions, many which developed in prison.

China's campaign to discredit Cao Shunli even continued past her death. Authorities continue to deny her family the dignity of releasing her body for burial. Chinese diplomats in Geneva objected to a planned moment of silence at the UN Human Rights Council.

It is a sad irony that Cao Shunli's pleas for human rights in China were finally heard at the UN after her death.

Cao Shunli is exactly the type of person the Chinese government should embrace—not jail, discredit, and leave to die. She was a brave advocate for human rights, who had sacrificed much to make her country a better place. She wanted a China that fulfilled its highest ideals and its promises to advance human rights and protect the poor and vulnerable.

Unfortunately, her case is not an isolated one.

President Xi Jinping has presided over one of the most extensive crackdowns on rights advocates in recent memory. 200 hundred people have been arrested in the past year and many more are intimidated into silence.

Chinese authorities are not only arresting rights advocates, they are also intimidating and detaining their family members as well—a chilling escalation of abuse that is both outrageous and illegal.

The Congress has repeatedly expressed its concern about health and welfare of Chen Kegui , the nephew of Chen Guangcheng and Liu Xia the wife of Nobel Prize Laureate, Liu Xiaobo —but many more families suffer in silence. We urge the Chinese government to stop its harassment and detention of the family members of dissidents.

We are also concerned about recent efforts to silence the work of human rights lawyers. Four lawyers were detained recently in northern China for seeking to defend Falun Gong practitioners arbitrarily detained in a "black jail." Over the past several years, human rights lawyers are often stripped of their legal licenses, beaten by police or hired "thugs," and detained—for seeking to provide legal services consistent with China's own laws and its international obligations.

China's human rights lawyers courageously remain committed to the rule-of-law, even though, it seems, the Chinese government is not.

China's active repression of ethnic minority communities has failed to bring stability and only created more discontent. It even jails those, like the Uyghur Ilham Tohti who seek to bridge the divide between their ethnic group and China's majority Han population, promoting inter-ethnic dialogue and understanding.

Expanding police power is not the answer to creating stability in restive ethnic minority areas of China. Tibetans, Uyghurs , and Mongolians should be given a way to shape policies that affect them and preserve and practice, without interference, their unique religions, cultures, and languages. Unfortunately, China has worked to silence Tohti's voice, and the voice of others, who have actively worked to ease inter-ethnic strains. The silencing of these voices is likely to further marginalize ethnic communities and worsen the prospects for peace and prosperity for Han and Uyghur alike.

President Xi came to office one year ago promising reforms of longstanding policies, including abolishing the re-education through labor (RTL) system of arbitrary detention, changing the household registration system and "One-Child" policy, and expanding efforts to stamp out corruption.

Yet, except for aggressive campaigns to discredit former political opponents and silence rights advocates, none of these reforms have produced results.

President Xi promised to create a "China Dream" of unlimited prosperity and progress, but coupled that with vision with a more conservative tone, opposing greater press freedom and "western-style" rule of law and extending existing curbs on the freedoms of expression, association, assembly, and religion. The Chinese government continues to prohibit independent labor unions and human rights organizations; heavily censors the media, the Internet, and academic research on topics deemed too "political." It uses "social stability" to justify suppression of human rights advocates and repressive policies in ethnic minority areas of Tibet, Xinjiang, and Inner Mongolia.

The China Dream is becoming a nightmare for those peacefully advocating for human rights and the rule of law.

A strong and secure China would welcome independent civil society and free press, committed to holding the Chinese government accountable to its highest ideals and promises. Instead it criminalizes dissenting opinions and uses repression to silence those viewed as challenging its authority.

China must begin to embrace the idea that continued prosperity and security can only be ensured when freedom is embraced and human rights protected.

The China Commission has repeatedly urged the Administration to raise, in a serious and visible way, the issue of human rights abuses in China. That need continues now, more than ever, in the midst of the current crackdown on rights defenders.

But more needs to be done to improve human rights diplomacy with China. The Administration has promised an "Asia Pivot," but the human rights and democracy pillar of that policy is, by far, the least developed part.

There are pressing economic and security concerns in the Pacific that require U.S. leadership, but the hard won truth of history is that a future of stability and prosperity is built on the foundation of liberty and human rights.

The United States must find credible ways to advance this principle in its relations with China. And, we must find ways to effectively link U.S. interests in human rights with its interests in global security and freer and fairer trade.

That is the challenge. We in the Congress, and at the CECC, promise to continue work to advance universally-recognized rights and freedoms in China.

○